The Seven Wonders of the Ancient World

By Charles River Editors

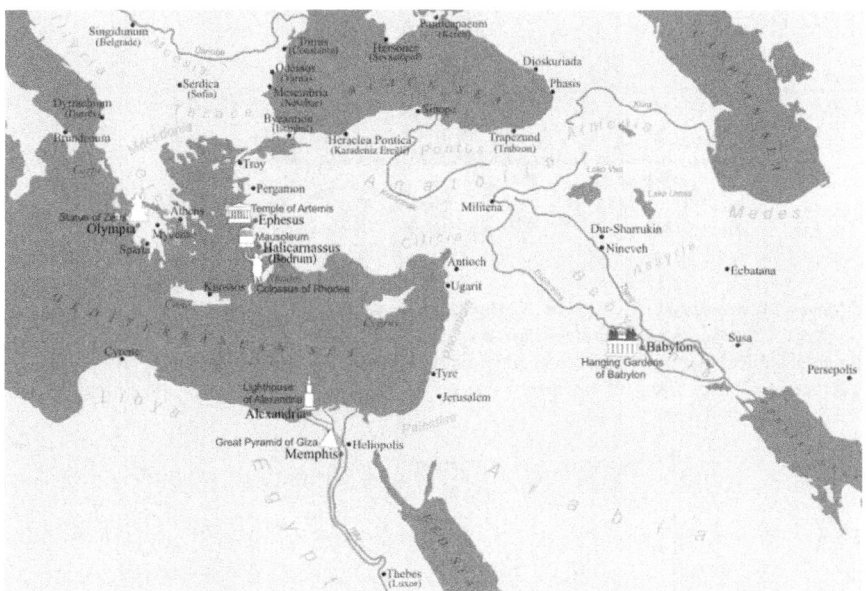

Map showing the locations of the Seven Wonders of the Ancient World

About Charles River Editors

Charles River Editors was founded by Harvard and MIT alumni to provide superior editing and original writing services, with the expertise to create digital content for publishers across a vast range of subject matter. In addition to providing original digital content for third party publishers, Charles River Editors republishes civilization's greatest literary works, bringing them to a new generation via ebooks.

Visit charlesrivereditors.com for more information.

Introduction

Engravings depicting the Seven Wonders of the Ancient World

The Seven Wonders of the Ancient World

"I have gazed on the walls of impregnable Babylon along which chariots may race, and on the Zeus by the banks of the Alpheus, I have seen the hanging gardens, and the Colossus of the Helios, the great man-made mountains of the lofty pyramids, and the gigantic tomb of Mausolus; but when I saw the sacred house of Artemis that towers to the clouds, the others were placed in the shade, for the sun himself has never looked upon its equal outside Olympus." - Antipater

Over 2,000 years ago, two ancient writers named Antipater of Sidon and Philo of Byzantium authored antiquity's most well known tour guides. After the two Greeks had traveled around the Mediterranean, they wrote of what they considered to be the classical world's greatest construction projects. While there is still some question as to who actually authored the text attributed to Philo and when it was authored, their lists ended up comprising the Seven Wonders of the Ancient World, igniting interest in the ones they chose and inspiring subsequent generations to identify their era's own Seven Wonders.

Naturally, the Seven Wonders of the Ancient World may be considered something of a misnomer. Only one still stands (the' Great Pyramid at Giza in Egypt), all existed in the Hellenistic culture rather than all over the world, and relatively few people saw them or visited them. They were all architectural marvels of the late Classical period and all but two were created by the Greeks. All but one were in the Mediterranean area. Even so, they represented a widespread range of works and cultures and spread out across three different continents.

The Seven Wonders of the Ancient World have continued to fascinate modern society, thanks in large measure to what was written about them and the fact that only one, the Great Pyramid at Giza, still survives. For that reason, speculation has revolved around the ones that didn't. Did the Colossus of Rhodes straddle the entire harbor or was it a statue on a pedestal at the mouth of the harbor, like an ancient Statue of Liberty? How did the Babylonians successfully plant and irrigate the Hanging Gardens? How tall was the Lighthouse of Alexandria? When did Phidias construct the Statue of Zeus at Olympia?

The Seven Wonders of the Ancient World profiles each of the seven wonders named by Philon, discussing the history of each wonder, what was written about each wonder, what is known about each wonder, and the lingering mysteries surrounding what is not known about them. Along with historic depictions of the wonders, you will learn about the Seven Wonders of the Ancient World like you never have before, in no time at all.

Becoming the 7 Wonders of the Ancient World

The Wonders were originally called "*theamata*" (things to be seen) and later "*thaumata*" (wonders) by the Greeks. The number seven was likely chosen because it had magical significance throughout the ancient Mediterranean, where numerology was studied as a body of knowledge. It also appears as a number of divine significance in the Bible, where it represents spiritual completion and perfection. The idea of wonders of the world first grew up in handbooks being written in the second and first centuries B.C. for Hellenic tourists. By this time in history, Greek culture had spread far enough (thanks to the conquests of Alexander in the latter half of the third century B.C.), naval and road technology was sufficiently advanced, and some Greeks were rich enough, that a small but significant percentage of the Greeks traveled. The rise of the Roman Empire, which eventually spread through most of the areas that contained the Wonders, made travel even easier and encouraged tourism, keeping these handbooks popular. After Rome fell, some of the Wonders still existed, so their memories as Wonders were preserved by succeeding cultures.

Originally, the number and identity of Wonders varied. The idea of there being seven came from the poet Antipater of Sidon, who wrote his tourist handbook circa 140 B.C. This was an historical list for Antipater, rather than a list of works in existence during his lifetime. Two Wonders (the Hanging Gardens of Babylon and the Colossus at Rhodes) no longer existed by his time, and another (the Temple of Artemis at Ephesus) had already been destroyed and rebuilt once. He listed the Wonders in a short section of a poem, choosing the Temple of Artemis as his favorite. Antipater's list eventually became the standard.

Antipater's Seven Wonders were the Great Pyramid of Giza, the Hanging Gardens of Babylon, the Temple of Artemis at Ephesus, the Statue of Zeus at Olympia, the Mausoleum at Halicarnassus, the Colossus at Rhodes, and the Lighthouse of Alexandria. Aside from the Great Pyramid, all were built between the seventh and third centuries B.C. Three were destroyed in antiquity, while three others beside the Great Pyramid survived into the Middle Ages.

Unlike later civilizations, which chose smaller works of art like paintings and sculptures for wonders, the Seven Wonders were all architectural masterpieces. This may be partly due to fact the list supposedly came down first from a third century B.C. engineer, Philo of Byzantium, who was fascinated by inventions, but it is also widely believed by historians and scholars that the text attributed to Philo was actually published nearly 1,000 years after his death. Two were statues, two were mausoleums, one was a temple, one a garden, and one a lighthouse. In most cases, they were notable for being unique, uniquely useful, or the largest of their kind. The people who built them and first wrote about them as Wonders were unaware of earlier Wonders like the cave art of the Paleolithic, the outdoor rock carvings of the Mesolithic, and the Neolithic stone tombs of northern Europe, a result of the fact that most of these prehistoric Wonders were either hidden or far from the Hellenistic World. The Greeks were also unaware of marvels in other lands like the Great Wall of China, which dates to the same time. Certain Bronze Age Wonders that they remembered in legendary form, such as the walls of Troy or the palace of Knossos on Crete, they ignored. All of the Wonders on the list were ones that the Greeks could still see, if only in ruin, and that can still be generally located today. A few have disappeared, but others still exist in a ruined state.

The Great Pyramid of Giza

One of the great ironies of the Seven Wonders is that the oldest of them (Khufu's Pyramid) is also the only surviving intact one. The Great Pyramid at Giza really belongs in its own class, since it comes from a much older culture than that of the Greeks. The Greeks had barely passed from the Neolithic into the Early Bronze Age when Khufu had his pyramid built circa 2560 B.C. near Memphis, just southwest of the Nile Delta in Egypt.

Egypt was the first civilization with organized written records (in close competition with Sumeria) and is also the oldest surviving one in the world. The same theocracy, with minor blips such as new dynasties, ruled Egypt from about 3050-30 B.C., when it officially became a province of the Roman Empire with the death of Cleopatra. The Egyptian religion that created the Pyramids endured until the sixth century A.D., even after Christianity had taken hold in the area, but Muslim invasions converted most of the population to Islam, which has persisted to the present day.

Unlike the ultimate fate of several other wonders, none of the subsequent invaders did much to the Pyramids, though the Great Sphinx nearby (also attributed to Khufu) suffered from vandalism over the centuries, particularly to its face.

The Great Pyramid is considered to be a Wonder collectively with several smaller pyramids in the area that were built for other pharaohs and their wives, all within the the same century. Khufu's Pyramid was originally 480 feet high, with a base nearly 750 feet wide, and it was reputedly designed by the Pharaoh's vizier, Hemon.

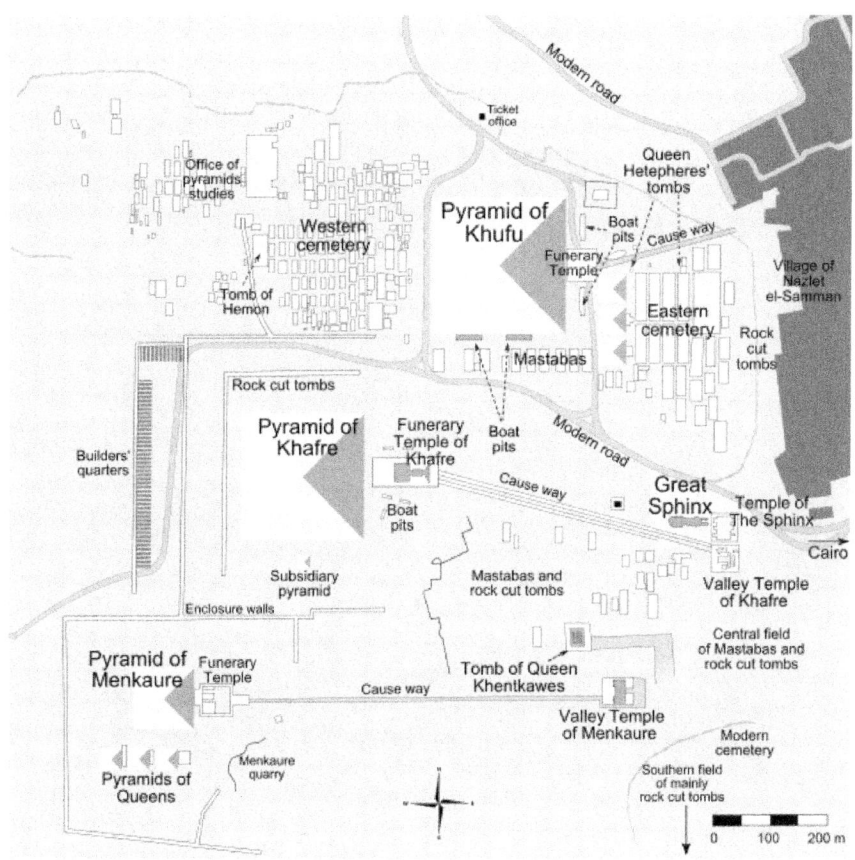

Map of the Giza Complex. Photo by Messer Woland

To say he had an ambitious project in mind would be a vast understatement. The construction of the Pyramid took 20 years, which sounds like a lengthy time until discovering how the rock for the pyramid was quarried and transported. The Great Pyramid is comprised of over 2 million limestone blocks, most of which were believed to have been transported from quarries near the site. But some of the pyramid's largest granited stones, weighing upwards of 80 tons, were moved 500 miles up or down the Nile River, and the Egyptians had to use an estimated 500,000 tons of mortar to hold the rocks together. Moreover, even though it has eroded to the extent that it is currently about 450 feet high, it is still the largest of the Wonders and was the tallest building in the world until the Lincoln Cathedral surpassed it around the 14th century A.D.

Ivory idol of Khufu

Khufu's pyramid was an elaborate stone mausoleum, a huge grave, constructed from limestone blocks fit so closely together that there is still only an average space of 0.5 millimeters between them. The interior was finished with granite and contained three chambers. One was for the Pharaoh, one was for his wife, and one at the base was left unfinished. Khufu's was not the first pyramid, but it was the largest. It is also possible that Khufu had the enormous statue of the Sphinx built around the same time.

The Great Pyramid has survived intact due to the stability of its design, sheer size, and periodic burial in sand. The architectural form of the pyramid is so structurally sound that it has been created and used independently by civilizations all over the world, especially in South and Central America. Also of great help was the remarkable longevity of Egyptian civilization, which continued under the pharaohs for three millennia, with great continuity thereafter. The ancient monuments, though neglected and forgotten as they sank beneath the sands, were also often regarded with great awe, an awe that protected them.

The Great Pyramid was originally larger than it is now, having been covered by a layer of white limestone that later broke off in earthquakes and was cannibalized for other buildings. Khufu's burial chamber is in the center, though it has long since been pillaged and emptied. The Egyptians believed that mummifying the body could ensure life after death, so they would create a burial chamber that was like a room for a living person, including cheerful wall paintings giving the dead person instructions on how to proceed through the afterlife, as well as food and drink, bedding, toys for children, and work tools for men and women. All of this has long since been stolen or destroyed along with Khufu' mummy in the Great Pyramid, but intact chambers have been found in smaller pyramids and tombs. Also, some things were not stolen from the Great Pyramid, such as the Pharaoh's coffin, because they were too massive to be moved or even broken up. The Pyramids' distance from the usual urban centers also spared them from being plundered too much for building materials.

Theories vary greatly on the mysterious passages inside, especially because not all of them could fit a human, and these passages extend well into the Pyramid. Two such passages reach the surface near the top of the pyramid, but their purpose remains unknown.

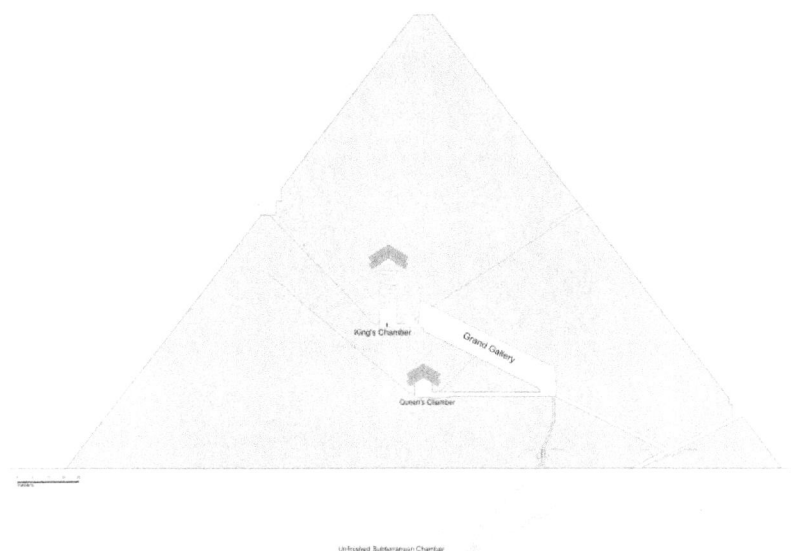

Equally mysterious is the way that the Pyramid was made, though archeologists have made much progress in this area over the past few decades. It is no longer believed, for example, that the Pyramids were built by slave labor (as the Ancient Greeks thought), due to excavations of nearby workers' cemeteries that were located by two archaeologists, one Egyptian (Zahi Hawass) and one American (Mark Lehner) in 1990. Instead, it appears the pyramids were built by skilled artisans and what appear to have been national levies of labor among the peasants. Enormous stones were lifted onto each other via ramps and rolling logs, a technique first reported by Greek historians Herodotus and Diodorus Siculus in ancient times and later confirmed by modern Egyptologists like Lehner and Roger Hopkins.

The Grand Gallery. Photo by Peter Prevos

One of the reasons why the Great Pyramid was not the first was because the artisans experimented over time with different styles and sizes, creating first step pyramids like the Pyramid of Saqqara (circa 2650 B.C.) and the Bent Pyramid (circa 2600 B.C.) and then the stable, smooth configuration of the Khufu Pyramid that became the model for later, smaller pyramids. It was apparently considered a great honor to work on this project because only the pharaohs had pyramid tombs and the Egyptians believed the pharaohs were gods on earth.

Despite being constructed about 4,500 years ago, the Great Pyramid was a huge endeavor and an architectural triumph that was never equaled or surpassed in Egypt, or by any other civilization that created pyramids. In the New Kingdom, the style turned instead to carving out tombs from the rock of what would later be known as the Valley of Kings.

The Hanging Gardens of Babylon

A 16th-century hand-coloured engraving of the "Hanging Gardens of Babylon" by Dutch artist Martin Heemskerck, with the Tower of Babel in the background

"There was also, beside the acropolis, the Hanging Garden, as it is called, which was built, not by Semiramis, but by a later Syrian king to please one of his concubines; for she, they say, being a Persian by race and longing for the meadows of her mountains, asked the king to imitate, through the artifice of a planted garden, the distinctive landscape of Persia. The park extended four plethra on each side, and since the approach to the garden sloped like a hillside and the several parts of the structure rose from one another tier on tier, the appearance of the whole resembled that of a theatre. When the ascending terraces had been built, there had been constructed beneath them galleries which carried the entire weight of the planted garden and rose little by little one above the other along the approach; and the uppermost gallery, which was fifty cubits high, bore the highest surface of the park, which was made level with the circuit wall of the battlements of the city. Furthermore, the walls, which had been constructed at great expense, were twenty-two feet thick, while the passage-way between each two walls was ten feet wide. The roof above these beams had first a layer of reeds laid in great quantities of bitumen, over this two courses of baked brick bonded by cement, and as a third layer of covering of lead, to the end that the moisture from the soil might not penetrate beneath. On all this again earth had been piled to a depth sufficient for the roots of the largest trees; and the ground, when levelled off, was thickly planted with trees of every kind that, by their great size or other charm, could give pleasure to the beholder. And since the galleries, each projecting beyond another, all received the light, they contained many royal lodgings of every description; and there was one gallery which contained openings leading from the topmost surface and machines for supplying the gardens with water, the machines raising the water in great abundance from the river, although no one outside could see it being done. Now this park, as I have said, was a later construction." - Diodorus Siculus

Like the Great Pyramid of Giza, the Hanging Gardens of Babylon came from an area of the world where the earliest civilizations grew up in a river valley. In Egypt, that river was the Nile, but in Babylon the two rivers were the Tigris and Euphrates (immortalized in the Bible as "the rivers of Babylon"). The Euphrates cut the city in half.

Babylon was the site of two relatively short-lived empires, the second of which is best remembered today for being the final destroyer of the nation of Israel, when it conquered the southern kingdom of Judea in 597 B.C. and brought that country's elite into exile. In 539 B.C., Babylon itself fell to the Persians, losing its own independence for good.

Civilization in Mesopotamia is extremely ancient, entering the Bronze Age—and recorded history—only a century and a half after the dawn of Egyptian civilization. Akkad, the third-millennium successor to Mesopotamia's first nation, Sumer, and predecessor to Babylon, may have been the world's first empire. Therefore, though the area was very politically unstable, with much destruction and discontinuity, it was also steeped in both agriculture and culture. This city was the site of the famous code of Hammurabi (circa 1792-1750 B.C.), Babylon's most powerful ruler, as well as the Hanging Gardens, themselves.

Ancient depiction of Hammurabi

The Hanging Gardens, like the Great Pyramid of Giza, were both a technological marvel and an aesthetic masterpiece. They were possibly constructed around the seventh century B.C., after the second rise of Babylon, making them the second-oldest of the Wonders. Reputedly, they were created by the biblical Nebuchadnezzar II (the king who conquered Judea) to please his homesick wife, after the model of Egyptian pleasure gardens. In 1993, British Assyriologist, Stephanie Dalley, proposed a theory that they were ordered built by the Assyrian King Sennacherib a century earlier for his giant palace at Nineveh, instead. She believed that the two sites were easily confused by ancient sources, resulting in the Gardens being incorrectly located in Babylon a century later.

Although there is still some question as to whether they ever truly existed, many ancient writers discussed the Hanging Gardens, including including Strabo, Diodorus Siculus, and Quintus Curtius Rufus. Moreover, Diodorus Siculus and Philo of Byzantium both described the mechanisms of the Gardens at length. According to their accounts, the Hanging Gardens were terraced and cultivated orchards that were built over a series of buildings made of glazed ceramic and perhaps watered by some kind of pulley or pump system of irrigation. Water was drawn from a reservoir through a network of reeds and bricks, held together by asphalt and cement, with lead used as a sealant. The Gardens were built on a citadel 80 feet high with walls 22 feet thick. The text attributed to Philo described the Hanging Gardens in detail:

> "The Hanging Gardens [is so-called because it] has plants cultivated at a height above ground level, and the roots of the trees are embedded in an upper terrace rather than in the earth. This is the technique of its construction. The whole mass is supported on stone columns, so that the entire underlying space is occupied by carved column bases. The columns carry beams set at very narrow intervals. The beams are palm trunks, for this type of wood – unlike all others – does not rot and, when it is damp and subjected to heavy pressure, it curves upwards. Moreover it does itself give nourishment to the root branches and fibres, since it admits extraneous matter into its folds and crevices. This structure supports an extensive and deep mass of earth, in which are planted broad-leaved trees of the sort that are commonly found in gardens, a wide variety of flowers of all species and, in brief, everything that is most agreeable to the eye and conducive to the enjoyment of pleasure. The whole area is ploughed in just the same way as solid ground, and is just as suitable as other soil for grafting and propagation. Thus it happens that a ploughed field lies above the heads of those who walk between the columns below. Yet while the upper surface of the earth is trampled underfoot, the lower and denser soil closest to the supporting framework remains undisturbed and virgin. Streams of water emerging from elevated sources flow partly in a straight line down sloping channels, and are partly forced upwards through bends and spirals to gush out higher up, being impelled through the twists of these devices by mechanical forces. So, brought together in frequent and plentiful outlets at a high level, these waters irrigate the whole garden, saturating the deep roots of the plants and keeping the whole area of cultivation continually moist. Hence the grass is permanently green, and the leaves of trees grow firmly attached to supple branches, and increasing in size and succulence with the constant humidity. For the root [system] is kept saturated and sucks up the all-pervading supply of water, wandering in interlaced channels beneath the ground, and securely maintaining the well-established and excellent quality of trees. This is a work of art of royal luxury [lit. 'riotous living'], and its most striking feature is that the labor of cultivation is suspended above the heads of the spectators."

Due to the different levels that the water had to be carried up in order to maintain them, and the fact that this was accomplished over the course of several centuries, the Hanging Gardens and the manner in which it was irrigated would have definitely represented one of antiquity's greatest technological marvels. The creation and sustenance of the Hanging Gardens would be made all the more amazing by the fact that they were being kept in such a hot and dry climate, no doubt providing a startling sight that would stand out even in one of antiquity's great cities. In fact, the descriptions provided by ancient writers indicates that water was transported upwards by something resembling an Archimedes screw (which was only known to have existed in the ancient world around the 3rd century B.C.), and estimates based on their descriptions suggest irrigating the Hanging Gardens would've required over 8,000 gallons of water per day.

On the one hand, several ancient historians provided detailed accounts of the size of the Hanging Gardens and their particulars. On the other, the sheer amount of water required and the fact that they would've required technology that was supposedly invented 400 years down the line cast doubt upon their existence. Officially, the reason why it is not known whether the Hanging Gardens ever existed is because they were reported to have been destroyed by several earthquakes, the last of which left the Hanging Gardens completely ruined by the second century B.C., around the time the Greek "tourists" were writing their pamphlets. Therefore, it is not known if any of the writers who described them ever saw the true Hanging Gardens, and though ancient Greeks and Romans of different centuries wrote about the Hanging Gardens and relied on previous ancient texts, Babylonian sources do not mention them. Neither do near-contemporaneous Greek sources like Herodotus. Unlike the Great Pyramid of Khufu, the Gardens do not survive, even in ruined form, though there have been theories about this or that set of ruins being the site of where they were built.

The Temple of Artemis at Ephesus

Model of Temple of Artemis, Miniatürk Park, Istanbul, Turkey. Photo by Zee Prime

"I have set eyes on the wall of lofty Babylon on which is a road for chariots, and the statue of Zeus by the Alpheus, and the hanging gardens, and the colossus of the Sun, and the huge labour of the high pyramids, and the vast tomb of Mausolus; but when I saw the house of Artemis that mounted to the clouds, those other marvels lost their brilliancy, and I said, "Lo, apart from Olympus, the Sun never looked on aught so grand". - Antipater

The next oldest of the Wonders was the Temple of Artemis in the city of Ephesus, on the western coast of Lydia (Anatolia, in what is now Turkey). It was also the oldest of the Greek Wonders. Construction began around 541 B.C. and took 10 years.

Unlike the other wonders, the enormous structure now described as a Wonder had two lives and two deaths. The first time it was destroyed, an arsonist named Herostratus burned it down in 358 B.C., in the (apparently accurate) belief that such destruction would make him famous. The city's inhabitants promptly executed him and made it illegal to mention his name thereafter, but the gossipy fourth century Greek historian Theopompus recorded the deed in his book, *The*

Hellenics, anyway. Oddly enough, ancient historians noted that the burning coincided with the birth of Alexander the Great, and Plutarch credits the destruction of the temple with the fact that Artemis was too preoccupied with Alexander's birth to save her own temple.

The Temple itself was first reputedly built by the king, Croesus, around 550 B.C., constructed of marble in replacement of a previous structure that had been destroyed by a flood. Third-century Hellenic African scholar, Callimachus of Cyrene, believed the older structure had been built by the Amazons, but the original Temple of Artemis actually dated back to the late Greek Bronze Age around 1,000 B.C. It may have been the first columned temple of its kind, but the site was not considered a Wonder of the World until after Croesus' version was built.

A lot of information about the history of the Temple of Artemis remains unknown. It was built three times in all before its final destruction by the Goths in 262 A.D., but the site's history thereafter is unclear before its rediscovery in 1869. It may have been repaired after the third century A.D., but this did not prevent it from being pillaged for building materials to construct Christian buildings in Constantinople a couple of centuries later. Early Christians resented the temple because of its cult and following. Stories in the New Testament survive of early saints praying to exorcise it, causing physical destruction, or being forbidden from entering the city due to citizens' fears of damage to the temple. These tales may reflect real-life instances of attempted arson or vandalism.

Croesus' temple was an enormous building for its time, being about 430 feet long and nearly 60 feet tall with 127 marble columns. It had a cedar ceiling and doors made of cypress. Dedicated to Artemis, the virgin Greek goddess of the hunt, who was later conflated with the Roman goddess Diana, Ephesus and its amazing temple were the center of the cult of Artemis throughout the Greek world, and the Ephesians considered her *their* goddess, resenting any claims by foreigners to her origins. This version of Artemis, in fact, predated Hellenic civilization, and she was noted for her fertility even more than her virginity.

Within the temple, the statue of Artemis was made of wood and kept covered by jewelry. It also either had many breasts, or was hung with eggs or bull testicles, depending on the source. Her image was carried through the streets during the Artemisia festival, much the way saints' images are carried through the streets on holy days in Catholic countries. The image is even described in the Book of Acts in the Bible as having fallen down from the sky. The festival was universal to the Greeks, not unlike the Olympics, though the Artemisia festival was intended to promote marriage rather than physical prowess, with young men and women seeking out spouses during it. The Goddess was served by a number of priestesses, many of them slaves and/or virgins.

The Lady of Ephesus, 1st century AD (Ephesus Archaeological Museum)

Much more is known of the Temple of Artemis than of some other Wonders because its foundations have survived and have been excavated. It was the favorite Wonder of Antipater of Sidon, who recorded a kind of religious epiphany in his brief description of it. It also inspired many copies, both in the Classical and Neo-Classical period. The insistence on rebuilding it in a place prone to destructive floods indicates that the site was extremely important to the worshipers of Artemis' cult, though Roman historian Pliny the Elder suggested a more practical reason for the site. He claimed that the Temple was built on wetlands to avoid being destroyed by earthquakes. This does not explain the insistence on building there after destruction by so many floods, but it may explain the original decision to select the site. The Mediterranean basin, and Anatolia especially, is prone to violent earthquakes. Most of the Wonders suffered damage from quakes and some were even destroyed outright.

Drum from the base of a column from the 4th-century rebuilding.

Another indication of the Temple and the site's local importance was that the Ephesians so resented the intrusions of Persian worship into the temple after the defeat of Croesus by Cyrus the Great in 547 B.C. that they politely refused Alexander's help and money in the fourth century to rebuild it. They may also have been motivated by the coincidence that Herostratus burned the building the same night that Alexander was born.

The civic identity of Ephesus appears to have been tied up with the welfare of the Temple. Once it burned and was apparently abandoned, Ephesus also faded in prestige and lost its central place in the religion of the Greco-Roman world.

The site of the Temple of Artemis today. Photo by Adam Carr

The Statue of Zeus at Olympia

16th century depiction of the Statue of Zeus at Olympia

"[Caligula] gave orders that such statues of the gods as were especially famous for their sanctity or for their artistic merit, including that of Zeus at Olympia, should be brought from Greece, in order to remove their heads and put his own in their place." – Suetonius

An indication of the widespread nature of the Hellenic world is that only two of the Wonders were found in Greece. One of these was the statue of Zeus at Olympia, a shrine in Elis on the edge of the Peloponnese region in southern Greece. As the city's name hints, the Olympic Games were held there from the eighth century B.C. onward, and the first of them was dedicated to Zeus. Unsurprisingly, Zeus was the primary deity worshiped in Olympia and temples there included two major structures dedicated separately to Zeus and his wife, Hera.

The statue of Zeus at Olympia was built earlier than the Colossus and also lasted longer, but it would eventually become an indirect victim of the change from pagan to Christian worship.

The work was not made of stone, but of ivory over wood and gold plated on bronze. Ivory was a common material used for sculpture in the ancient world, and its combination with gold was a very popular and archaic form of statuary known as "chryselephantine" that was commonly used for oversized cult statues, perhaps because it was relatively light compared to stone. The statue of Zeus was nearly 40 feet tall and portrayed Zeus seated on a jewel-inlaid throne, probably in a position similar to the famous statue of Abraham Lincoln in the Lincoln Memorial in Washington, D.C. It was also reported that Zeus held a small statue of Nike (the Greek goddess of Victory) in his right hand and a gold-inlaid staff, topped with a gold eagle, in his left.

A temple was constructed just to house the statue, and some reported that it was lit by fire inside the windowless temple, making the statue of Zeus a mysterious and imposing sight. To get an idea of just how large and imposing the statue itself was, ancient historian Strabo wrote, "It seems that if Zeus were to stand up, he would unroof the temple." It inspired awe in others who saw it as well; Plutarch wrote in his Life of Paulus that when the Roman general saw the statue, he was "was moved to his soul, as if he had seen the god in person." 1st century A.D. Greek orator Dio Chrysostom said seeing the statue could make a man forget all his troubles.

Chryselephantine statuary is quite ancient, going back almost four thousand years, and it was especially popular in Greece during the Archaic period (800-480 B.C.), but the Zeus statue itself dates from the Classical period. Perhaps because of the antiquity of the art, but also because of the value of the materials, very few chryselephantine statues survive in more than fragmentary form. However, reconstructions like the one of Athena Parthenos found in the full-sized reconstruction of the Parthenon in Nashville, Tennessee indicate that the combination of ivory for the skin and gold for the clothing and armor, as well as their generally large size made these cult statues an impressive and intimidating sight.

The workshop of Phidias at Olympia

Because of the recent discovery of the nearby workshop of its creator, much is known about the Zeus statue's origins. Its sculptor was a Greek named Phidias, an Athenian of the Golden Age widely regarded as one of Ancient Greece's greatest sculptors, who created it around the middle of the fifth century B.C. One of the greatest in his art, Phidias also designed statues for the Parthenon, including the Athena Parthenos, as well as a colossal bronze sister statue outside, the Athena Promanchos, which was eventually carried off to Constantinople and destroyed there by a Christian mob over 1500 years later.

Despite his fame as a sculptor, Phidias was twice accused of stealing precious materials from one of his works and eventually died in prison around 430 B.C. None of his works survive, except in the form of much-later (and smaller) Roman copies. The Zeus statue does not survive in any form save some designs on coins and carved jewels. Though the richness of the materials that he used perhaps contributed to this destruction, some of Phidias' works survived well into the Middle Ages, even after being transported thousands of miles from their original destinations.

Stories vary on how the statue of Zeus was destroyed. According to the gossipy Roman historian Suetonius (circa 69-140 A.D.), it was nearly removed and defaced in the first part of the first century A.D. when the Roman Emperor Caligula ordered all especially holy statues in the Roman Empire to be dismantled and taken to Rome so that their heads could be replaced with sculptures of his own head. According to the ancient Roman, the statue of Zeus was spared by a miracle, the convenient assassination of Caligula in 41 A.D. According to Suetonius, the statue of Zeus foretold the coming assassination by laughing and frightening off the workmen

The statue was still in good condition in the second century A.D. when the historian, Pausanius, gave the detailed eyewitness description of it that has come down to us. Sometime in the fifth century, however, it disappeared from Olympia. Seven centuries later, Byzantine historian Georgios Kedrenos claimed that it was removed to Constantinople, like the Athena statues, where it was destroyed in a great fire that burned most of that city in 475 A.D. However, it is also possible that it was never moved and was destroyed when the temple housing it burned around 425 A.D.

The Mausoleum at Halicarnassus

Model of the Mausoleum at Miniatuk Park in Istanbul, Turkey. Photo by Nevit Dilmen

The Mausoleum at Halicarnassus (later Bodrum, on the southern coast of Turkey) is another Classical Wonder of the World and also one from Anatolia, near the island of Rhodes. It was constructed around 350 B.C. for the Persian king and satrap (a type of subject king in the Persian Empire) Mausolus, and his wife (and sister) Artemisia II of Caria. Since the Mausoleum was not completed until after her death, it is believed that Artemisia oversaw most of the construction after her husband's death in 353 and may even have commissioned it herself. It was said that her grief over losing him was so extreme that she drank his ashes every day, and her husband's name later gave the English language the word "mausoleum" to describe an elaborately constructed tomb. The structure was perceived by the Greeks as a symbol of spousal love and devotion similar to the way modern tourists perceive the Taj Mahal in India.

Like the Temple of Artemis, the Mausoleum at Halicarnassus was huge for its type of building, being about 150 feet tall and possessing 36 columns of marble on its four sides, nine to a side. Also like the Temple of Artemis, the site of the Mausoleum includes ruins that have been excavated in modern times. Using this, an accurate scale replica has been successfully constructed in Istanbul, Turkey, and pieces of the beautiful sculpture on the Mausoleum have been retrieved. Therefore, it is one of the few Wonders that survived in some form and have directly inspired modern artists and architects.

The Mausoleum site today

The Mausoleum was not the work of a single sculptor but of five, making it a model of Classical sculpture. Despite being Persian and from Caria, far from Greece, Mausolus was an admirer of Hellenistic culture, and the Mausoleum represented a masterpiece of Greek art designed by two Greek architects, Satyros and Pythius of Priene. Pythius, especially, preferred the graceful Ionic columns popular in Asia Minor to the stockier Doric columns, and his lost

Commentaries, which subsequent writers cited, discussed his architectural theories. A small plaque from a temple he built for Athena survives in the British Museum. Four sculptors each carved a wall of the Mausoleum—Leochares of Athens, Bryaxis, Scopas of Paros and his rival Timotheus. Roman copies of their works in other places survive and are considered influential masterpieces on later art. A fifth artist, Pteron, made a crown for the Mausoleum after Artemisia's death, followed by Pythius, again, who created a quadriga—a marble statue of a chariot and horses--atop the crown. These men were at the very top of their craft and might never have willingly worked on a single project together. In addition, this is the only known major architectural Hellenistic work devoted to a secular theme (the burial of two mortals) rather than religious art dedicated to the Greek pantheon. The themes of the carvings included many mythical enemies of the Greeks, such as the Amazons and centaurs.

The architecture was a marvel of engineering that was copied by neo-Classical buildings. The ultimate fate of the Mausoleum itself is unknown, though it was known to have survived the city's conquest by Alexander the Great in 334 B.C. intact. Pirates who occupied the city in the first century B.C. also left it unharmed, and though a series of earthquakes had reduced it to foundations by the 15th century A.D., it was still intact enough to be considered a "wonder" by a Christian pilgrim, the Archbishop Eustathius of Thessalonica, in the 12th century.

A sculpture of the lion from the Mausoleum now at the British Museum.

Unfortunately, the arrival of the Knights of St. John (the Hospitallers) in Rhodes and Bodrum proved ill for the great structure. They used materials from it to reinforce their castle at Bodrum when it was threatened by the Turks in 1522 and burned the marble for lime, though they did retrieve and install the best of the sculptures in their castle. The burial chamber of Mausolus and Artemisia, which had been underground, was also looted at some point over the centuries, though husband and wife were likely cremated in the Greek fashion and buried in urns. The famous marbles were also looted in the 19th century during a three-year expedition by English archeologist Sir Charles Thomas Newton and carted off to the British Museum. Even so, an expedition in the 1970s by Danish archeologist Professor Kristian Jeppesen was able to reconstruct the foundations of the Mausoleum. Several structures such as American president Ulysses S. Grant's tomb in New York City and the Shrine of Remembrance in Melbourne, Australia have been inspired by this Wonder.

Grant's Tomb in New York

The Colossus at Rhodes

Drawing of Colossus of Rhodes, illustrated in the Grolier Society's 1911 Book of Knowledge

"Why man, he doth bestride the narrow world
Like a Colossus, and we petty men
Walk under his huge legs and peep about
To find ourselves dishonorable graves." – William Shakespeare, *Julius Caesar*

One of the youngest and most mysterious Wonders was the Colossus at Rhodes, and given that its lifespan was the shortest of the Wonders (about half a century), there is some question as to how many of those describing it had ever actually seen it. According to ancient accounts, it was a large, 110 foot tall bronze statue of a man, built around 292-80 B.C. to commemorate a great victory for Rhodes after they held off a siege of the city in 305 B.C.

According to legend, the Rhodians melted down the bronze from the abandoned siege equipment and built the Colossus next to their harbor's mouth, and it was so large that it could be seen for miles. Little is now known about its actual appearance—whether it was clothed, the hairstyle, or even its posture—but it was dedicated to the sun god Helios. Some (much later) portraits of it show it holding aloft a fiery torch, much like the Statue of Liberty, indicating it may also have had a somewhat practical purpose of guiding ships into the harbor, which had a rather narrow mouth.

19th century depiction of the Colossus of Rhodes

The Colossus appears to have been created by a process of building up an iron frame on stone feet and a nearly 50 foot platform, then fixing bronze plates to it (like the Statue of Liberty, which was a 19th century speculative copy of the Colossus). Scaffolding was built around it as the plates were built up toward the neck and head. When the Colossus was finished, it was dedicated, "To you, o Sun, the people of Dorian Rhodes set up this bronze statue reaching to Olympus, when they had pacified the waves of war and crowned their city with the spoils taken from the enemy. Not only over the seas but also on land did they kindle the lovely torch of freedom and independence. For to the descendants of Herakles belongs dominion over sea and land."

Given its design, when the earthquake that knocked it down struck in 226 B.C., historians theorize that the plates shook loose, arms first, and the statue fell in several pieces, leaving the feet and the base standing. There is also some debate as to its position and stance. Some medieval sources claimed that it was built to straddle the harbor, as immortalized in Shakespeare's play, *Julius Caesar*. However, there are two potential problems with this image. One is a case of stability, as the bronze statue would have fallen even more quickly than it did, under its own weight. Archaeologists also believe that making the statue straddle the harbor would have required closing the entire harbor during its construction, and the destruction of the statue would have blocked entrance to the harbor as well.

More evidence suggesting the statue did not straddle the harbor comes from eyewitness accounts about the remains of the statue, such as that of historians Strabo and Pliny the Elder. Though the statue was felled by an earthquake in the early third century, pieces of it stayed where they were for eight centuries, partly because the Rhodians did not have the heart to break them down and partly because they were perhaps too large to be moved. However, they were said to be on the banks of the harbor. If the statue had straddled the harbor mouth, the falling pieces would have choked the harbor and would have needed to be moved.

After an earthquake toppled the statue and devastated the city in 226 B.C., the pieces remained for quite a long time before they were finally hauled off after the Muslim conquest of Rhodes. Eighth century Byzantine monk Theophanes Confessor claimed that the Muslim army sold off the pieces in 654 A.D. to a "Jewish merchant of Edessa," though this story may be a literary invention intended to foretell the coming Apocalypse. It is also possible that the Knights of St. John, who held the island in the late Middle Ages, broke down the pieces and used the still-valuable bronze for scrap. At any rate, no remaining pieces have yet been discovered in modern times, so both the site and the appearance of the statue remain a mystery. Some have even speculated that it actually stood atop Rhodes' acropolis, not at the mouth of the harbor.

Though it was ultimately too experimental to have survived long, the Colossus was a remarkable achievement for the Greeks and drew much attention from Greek historians. Even those visiting after it had fallen were struck with awe at the sight of the ruins, and the ruins themselves were a tourist destination. Pliny the Elder wrote that each of the statue's fingers were larger than most statues. Not surprisingly, the Colossus has lent its name through the passage of time as a description for any large object.

The Lighthouse of Alexandria

Computer model rendition of the Lighthouse of Alexandria, by Emad Victor Shenouda

"The Pharos rises at the end of the island. The building is square, about 8.5 metres (28 ft) each side. The sea surrounds the Pharos except on the east and south sides. This platform measures, along its sides, from the tip, down to the foot of the Pharos walls, 6.5 metres (21 ft) in height. However, on the sea side, it is larger because of the construction and is steeply inclined like the side of a mountain. As the height of the platform increases towards the walls of the Pharos its width narrows until it arrives at the measurements above. ... The doorway to the Pharos is high up. A ramp about 183 metres (600 ft) long used to lead up to it. This ramp rests on a series of curved arches; my companion got beneath one of the arches and stretched out his arms but he was not able to reach the sides. There are 16 of these arches, each gradually getting higher until the doorway is reached, the last one being especially high." - Abou Haggag Youssef Ibn el-Andaloussi, circa 1165 A.D.

The youngest of the Wonders also turned out to be the most practical and one of the longest-lived, surviving into the late Middle Ages. It was a lighthouse built on the northern coast of Egypt in Africa, at the Greek city founded in Alexander's name. It was the Pharos, the Great Lighthouse of Alexandria.

The Pharos Lighthouse was built in the third century B.C. under the orders of Ptolemy I, about thirty years after the founding of Alexandria in 332 B.C.. Alexandria had been carefully situated by Alexander and his engineers on a natural harbor on the western side of the marshy Nile Delta on the northern coast of Egypt. This avoided the diseases of the marshlands (such as malaria) and ensured solid ground on which to build, while still giving access to a water source and transportation. The city still exists today and is a thriving metropolis, though most of the ancient city has sunk beneath the Mediterranean.

The island of Pharos, on which the Lighthouse was built, had a notorious reputation that influenced the building of the Lighthouse. The Lighthouse was not built to warn mariners from shoals, but to ward off piracy. Up to that time, according to first century B.C. Greek historians like Diodorus Siculus (of Sicily) and Strabo, Pharos had been a haven for pirates. The fourth century Hellenic tyrant, Dionysius I of Syracuse, cleaned the pirates out of the western Mediterranean and established a settlement at Pharos, but piracy quickly returned after his death. The establishment of the Lighthouse helped deter the pirates from reestablishing themselves on the island and threatening mariners or the nearby newly founded city.

Though the Lighthouse is long gone, historians and archeologists have been able to reconstruct it fairly well, due to descriptions and several surviving imitations. The Romans based a number of later lighthouses on its design, and Caesar himself wrote about it in his commentaries on the Civil War against Pompey the Great, ""Now because of the narrowness of the strait there can be no access by ship to the harbour without the consent of those who hold the Pharos. In view of this, Caesar took the precaution of landing his troops while the enemy was preoccupied with fighting, seized the Pharos and posted a garrison there. The result was that safe access was secured for his corn supplies and reinforcements." Also, a funerary monument, built around the same time as the lighthouse, the Pharos of Abusir, a town southwest of Alexandria, appears to have been modeled after it in a scaled-down fashion.

Pharos of Abusir. Photo by Gene Poole

As with most of his projects, Alexander did not live to see the lighthouse completed, and it was ordered finished by his successor in Egypt, his friend and general Ptolemy I Soter, who ruled as the first pharaoh of a new Greek dynasty that lasted until its final ruler, Cleopatra VII, committed suicide in 30 B.C. According to first century A.D. Roman historian Pliny the Elder (who perished in Pompeii after Mount Vesuvius erupted in the first century A.D.), the Pharos was designed by the Greek engineer, Sostratus of Knidos, though others claimed Sostratus only financed it. Regardless, it cost 800 talents, an enormous sum for that time. The following century, Roman satirist Lucian wrote that Sostratus was forbidden by Ptolemy's son, Ptolemy II, from signing the Pharos, but came up with a clever way of doing so, anyway. He had his name carved into the base and then covered with plaster. Long after both his and Ptolemy's deaths, the plaster wore away, exposing him as the architect.

The Lighthouse was described twice, by two Muslim travelers, Idrisi and Yusuf Ibn al-Shaikh, toward the end of its existence in the 10th century A.D. The best and most detailed description came from a still-later tourist, Abou Haggag Youssef Ibn el-Andaloussi, in 1165. He described the Pharos Lighthouse as being 300 cubits in height (140-183 meters or about 450-550 feet). The structure, which was constructed of marble blocks sealed together by lead mortar, was built differently than a modern lighthouse, which is a single cylindrical structure. The stone platform at the bottom was nearly 20 feet high, and on top of it was a base about 225 feet high and 100 feet wide. On it sat an octagonal tower over 100 feet high, and on top of that a cylinder about 60 feet wide. At the very top of the cylinder was a cupola that held the light (an open fire with, in some reports, a bronze mirror to reflect and concentrate the light) and was topped by a statue, reputedly of Poseidon, the god of the sea. Ancient coins showed statues at the top of the four corners of the base, possibly of another sea god, Triton, and excavation of similar statues from the Alexandrine harbor appears to support the existence of the Tritons.

A drawing of the lighthouse by German archaeologist Prof. H. Thiersch (1909)

Even more complex than the basic structure was the ingenious machinery used to keep it operational. The reflected light at the top of the lighthouse was reputed to be so powerful that it could be focused on distant ships to set them on fire, or as a reflector telescope to view distant Constantinople. These feats seem unlikely, since Constantinople was much farther distant than the 100 miles the lighthouse could be seen by mariners at night, and it almost certainly could not have refracted light with the intensity necessary to burn a ship. During the day, mariners could use the smoke from the fire for guidance.

While the lighthouse almost certainly served no purpose other than the one it was designed for, other descriptions about how it was operated are far more believable. Accounts claim that there was a nearly 600 foot long ramp built on 16 arches leading to a doorway partway up the lighthouse, and an internal spiral ramp large enough to accommodate animals dragging fuel in carts. Reports also mentioned a dumbwaiter for the purpose of bringing wood up to the top of the lighthouse to feed the fire. All of these measurements are approximate, since they were reported (like the Pyramids) in cubits, an ancient, biblical measurement of widely varying lengths, but they were far less ludicrous than other assertions about the use of the lighthouse.

The inventions ascribed to the Pharos Lighthouse were the most technologically advanced of the Seven Wonders, with the possible exception of the mysterious and perhaps legendary Hanging Gardens of Babylon, and they still seem incredible. However, none of them were beyond the abilities of the Greeks or Egyptians at that time. Archeologists have determined that the Egyptians used ramps in the building of the Pyramids some two thousand years before the building of the Lighthouse. An early step pyramid northwest of Memphis, the 4700-year-old Pyramid of Djoser, reached nearly 200 feet in height and could have inspired the builders of the Pharos Lighthouse. Another possible inspiration came from early ziggurats from Mesopotamia, from the same period as the Djoser Pyramid, which reached 100-175 feet in height.

As for the bronze mirror, polished bronze mirrors were commonly used in both Greek and Roman households, and optics in the form of quartz lens had been invented by the Egyptians and Mesopotamians around 700 B.C. Many Classical Greek scientists had fashioned scientific theories and work on optics around the time that the Lighthouse was built. Though the Pharos Lighthouse was the first recorded lighthouse (such that the island gave its name, "faros," to stand for "lighthouse" in Latin and Romance languages), the Romans later built over 30 lighthouses of similar design throughout the Roman Empire, such as the second century A.D. Tower of Hercules on the northwestern coast of Spain and another pair of first century A.D. lighthouses in Dover, England. Each of the inventions ascribed to the Great Lighthouse of Alexandria were individually possible.

The remarkable thing about the Lighthouse itself was that it appeared to be the first of its kind and also the largest, and that this was the first time anyone thought to put all of these inventions together into one building. Also remarkable was its longevity — fifteen centuries — though the Tower of Hercules has now lasted two centuries longer intact.

The Tower of Hercules. Photo by Alessio Damato

    The Pharos remained in operation for 15 centuries, though the fire was replaced with a mosque following the Muslim conquest of Egypt in the seventh century A.D. There are two possible reasons for its lengthy survival, and the fact that it wasn't destroyed by foreign conquest like some of its counterpart wonders. First, the solid construction of the lighthouse was not dissimilar to the sturdy construction of the Pyramids. It survived the conquest of the island by the Romans in 219 B.C., during a campaign to eliminate the Illyrian pirates who once again threatened Roman trade, and its great blocks kept it in place even when a tsunami struck it in 365 A.D. Second, the Pharos was both a useful warning to mariners and a very popular tourist spot. Its beauty drew visitors and entrepreneurs who served the visitors alike, and the octagonal tower was open to tourists, who appreciated the unique, high vantage point.

The Pharos' dual purpose ensured that it was carefully maintained, even when Hellenic and Roman infrastructure in the area receded and collapsed. What eventually brought down the Pharos was the same thing that brought down the Colossus at Rhodes: earthquakes. It was reportedly repaired in the 10th century A.D., reducing its height, due to cracks in the stone caused by an earthquake in 956. In 1303 and 1325, two earthquakes made the Pharos Lighthouse unusable and unable to be entered safely, according to another Muslim traveler, Ibn Battuta. The lighthouse finally came down in 1375, and the rubble remained visible until much of it was used in 1480 to create a nearby fortress by the Egyptian sultan, Qaitbay.

An apocryphal tale also claims that the Pharos Lighthouse was dismantled in 850 A.D. through trickery. A Byzantine emperor, seeking to rid the Mediterranean of rival ports, tricked the Caliph in Cairo into dismantling the Lighthouse under the impression that treasure lay beneath it. Once aware of the ruse, the Caliph attempted to rebuild the Lighthouse but was unsuccessful. However, this story is clearly belied by witness accounts in 1115 to the continued existence of the Pharos Lighthouse, as well as the continued success of Alexandria as a port.

A replica of the Lighthouse was constructed in China in 2005, and plans to rebuild the Lighthouse on Pharos (similar to proposals to rebuild the Colossus at Rhodes) have been raised by the Egyptian government in the past 30 years, though nothing so far as come of them. A recent expedition in underwater archeology by French archeologist Jean-Yves Empereur in 1994 found what are now believed to be blocks from the fallen Lighthouse in the harbor. The site has been explored and opened to scuba diving visitors. Though in a very different way from when Antipater of Sidon first saw it, the Pharos has become a tourist attraction and a Wonder again once more.

Conclusion

The Seven Wonders of the World were unique accomplishments, both for their time and for centuries thereafter. Some were so remarkable, and have since been so thoroughly destroyed, that they now seem legendary. One survives. Others have left behind remnants that confirm their unique beauty and inventiveness. These were all works that were created as the pinnacle, or even the foundation, of their craft. Ironically, they were never all in existence at the same time. By the time the Lighthouse at Pharos was built, the Colossus had fallen near the Rhodian harbor and the second Temple of Artemis had already burned down, while the Hanging Gardens were fading back into the desert. The Pyramid at Giza was likely covered with sand. It was not possible for any living tourist of any time to have seen all of the Wonders. In fact, by the time Antipater of Sidon wrote his handbook, three of the four Wonders were either in ruins or completely rebuilt, making his account of seeing them all somewhat fanciful. Yet, the memory of them persisted and was preserved. Other candidates, such as the walls of Babylon (which were confirmed to exist) were not retained.

In addition to being a Hellenistic list, the wonders that were included had several distinct features. For example, they represented starkly different technologies and art forms that were cutting edge for their time, having been constructed by very different people for quite different reasons—two as sepulchers, two to signal entrance to a harbor, two for love, two as places of worship, and so on. The wonders were constructed over a very long period, going back long before the relatively short Hellenistic Classical civilization, and they were constructed over a wide geographic range on three continents. And though five of them were constructed by Greeks (though it could be argued that the Lighthouse on Pharos was constructed in Egypt, using technology of largely Egyptian design), two were pre-Hellenistic and unrelated to the Greeks in any way. Another was constructed by a group of Greek artists under the direction of (and for) non-Greeks, who were, in fact, enemies of the Greek states.

Just as importantly, all of the Wonders inspired imitators and further inventions, influencing Hellenistic and post-Hellenistic civilizations long after their destruction. Though the Pyramid at Giza is the only one left standing, most of the Wonders still exist with us in some form and still serve as inspirations and tourist attractions, just as they did two thousand years ago. Perhaps it is not such a shock that Antipater chose to write about their ruins as if they were still in existence in his time, enough to attract tourists who found them worth the visit. After all, that is largely how we treat them today.

Online Information on the Seven Wonders of the Ancient World

The Pyramids at Giza

The Discovery of the Tombs of the Pyramid Builders at Giza
[http://www.guardians.net/hawass/buildtomb.htm]

How to Build a Pyramid [http://www.archaeology.org/0705/etc/pyramid.html]

The Hanging Gardens of Babylon

Ancient Mesopotamian Gardens and the Identification of the Hanging Gardens of Babylon Resolved:

[http://www.jstor.org/discover/10.2307/1587050?uid=3739256&uid=2&uid=4&sid=21100919498501]

Earthly Paradises: Ancient Gardens in History and Archaeology
[http://books.google.com/books?id=oHMxwLVbSDMC&pg=PA26#v=onepage&q&f=false]

The Temple of Artemis at Ephesus

Temple of Artemis [http://www.kusadasi.biz/historical-places/temple-of-artemis.html]

Temple of Artemision, Artemision Temple Ephesus [http://www.ephesus.us/ephesus/templeofartemis.htm]

The Statue of Zeus at Olympia

The Temple of Zeus [http://www.olympia-greece.org/templezeus.html]

The Temple of Zeus at Olympia [http://employees.oneonta.edu/farberas/arth/arth209/olympia_temp_zeus.html]

The Mausoleum at Halicarnassus

Mausoleum of Halicarnassus: The Full Story [http://www.bodrumpages.com/English/mausoleum.html]

The Mausoleum of Halicarnassus [http://www.livius.org/ha-hd/halicarnassus/halicarnassus_mausoleum.html]

The Colossus at Rhodes

The Colossus At Rhodes: A Wonder of the Ancient World [http://www.rhodesguide.com/rhodes/colossus_rhodes.php/]

How Stuff Works: The Colossus of Rhodes [http://history.howstuffworks.com/asian-history/seven-wonder-ancient-world6.htm]

The Lighthouse of Alexandria

The Great Lighthouse at Alexandria [http://www.unmuseum.org/pharos.htm]

A Brief History of Lighthouses [http://americanhistory.si.edu/collections/lighthouses/history.htm]

Printed in Great Britain
by Amazon